BATS SET II

SLIT-FACED BATS

Jill C. Wheeler
ABDO Publishing Company

visit us at
www.abdopub.com

Published by ABDO Publishing Company, 4940 Viking Drive, Edina, Minnesota 55435.
Copyright © 2006 by Abdo Consulting Group, Inc. International copyrights reserved in all
countries. No part of this book may be reproduced in any form without written permission from
the publisher. The Checkerboard Library™ is a trademark and logo of ABDO Publishing
Company.

Printed in the United States.

Cover Photo: Visuals Unlimited
Interior Photos: Animals Animals p. 13; © Merlin D. Tuttle, Bat Conservation
     International pp. 5, 9, 11, 17, 19, 21

Series Coordinator: Tamara L. Britton
Editors: Tamara L. Britton, Stephanie Hedlund
Art Direction, Maps, and Diagrams: Neil Klinepier

Library of Congress Cataloging-in-Publication Data

Wheeler, Jill C., 1964-
    Slit-faced bats / Jill C. Wheeler.
       p. cm. -- (Bats. Set II)
    Includes bibliographical references (p.) and index.
    ISBN 1-59679-323-6
     1. Nycteridae--Juvenile literature. I. Title.

QL737.C565W49 2005
599.4'9--dc22
                                                    2005045276

CONTENTS

SLIT-FACED BATS

Slit-faced bats are one of more than 900 **species** of bats. There are 13 species in their **family**. Bats are second only to rodents in their number of species.

Slit-faced bats have a slit that divides their **muzzle**. The slit creates a cavity in the bat's face. So, they are also called hollow-faced bats.

Like all bats, slit-faced bats are **mammals**. Humans are mammals, too. Mother bats produce milk to feed their young, just like human mothers. However, bats are the only mammals that can fly.

Many people think bats are scary or harmful. This is not true. Bats can be very helpful to humans. They eat many insect pests. Some bats also help **pollinate** plants or plant new trees. This makes bats and humans important partners in Earth's **ecosystem**.

Scientists are working to learn the function of the slit-faced bat's unusual facial structure.

WHERE THEY'RE FOUND

Bats can be found all around the world. They live everywhere except for some **isolated** islands, and the North and South poles.

Slit-faced bats live in many different regions. They can be found in Africa south of the Sahara Desert. In the Middle East, they live in the dry lands of Palestine and the Arabian Peninsula. They also live in Malaysia and around the islands of Indonesia.

Because they live in such a large area, slit-faced bats have many different **habitats**. Some **species** live in grasslands. Some live in scrub forests. Others live in moist forests, marshes, or swamps.

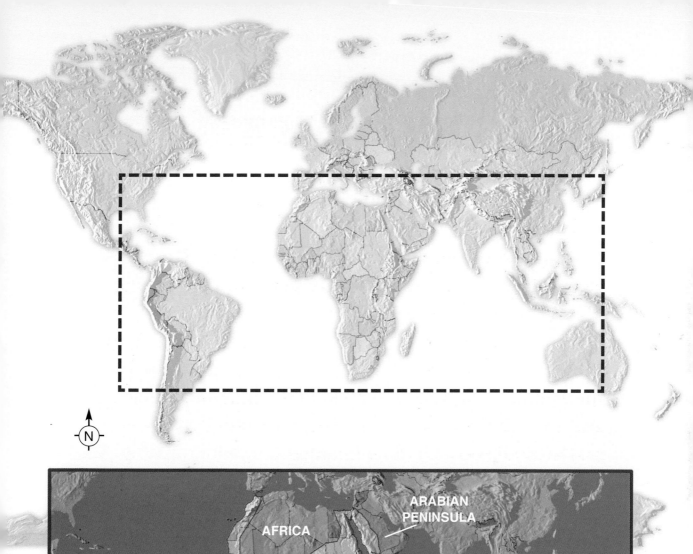

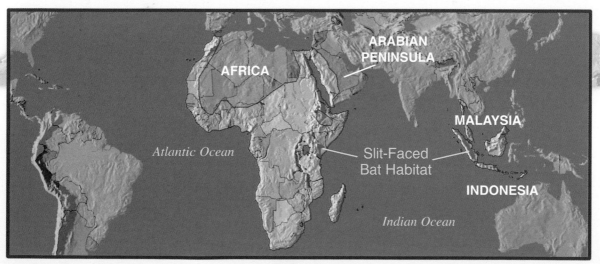

Where They Live

Like all bats, slit-faced bats are **nocturnal**. During the day, they need a place to sleep. They **roost** in roofs or empty rooms of houses. Outside, they live in caves, hollow trees, bushes, or on rock **outcroppings**.

Slit-faced bats have also been known to move into animal burrows. Aardvarks and porcupines have come home to find unwanted bat guests in their house! Slit-faced bats are very fond of their chosen roost. They will return to a place even if they are scared away from it.

Most slit-faced bats roost alone, in pairs, or in small **family** groups. Yet, some **species** like to live in colonies with other bats. One species gathers in groups of about 20 bats. Another can live with 500 to 600 bats in the same cave. Still others may live with thousands of bats.

This Dobson's slit-faced bat is roosting in a hollow tree.

SIZES

An amazing one-quarter of all **mammals** are bats. That's a lot of bats! These bats come in many different sizes.

The smallest bat is the bumblebee bat. It really is the size of a big bumblebee. The world's largest bats are the bat **family** called the flying foxes. The flying foxes are the world's largest flying mammals. Some **species** of flying foxes are more than 17 inches (43 cm) long. They can have a **wingspan** of more than 5 feet (1.5 m).

Slit-faced bats are medium-sized bats. Their bodies are between 3 and 7 inches (8 and 18 cm) long from head to tail. They weigh around one-third of an ounce to one ounce (10 to 30 g).

This Dobson's slit-faced bat has short, broad wings. They help the bat navigate through forests while hunting.

SHAPES

Slit-faced bats have short brown fur. The fur is darker on their back and lighter on their stomach. The bats have large ears and very small eyes.

The most distinct feature of the slit-faced bat is its face. A slit runs from a pit in the middle of the bat's forehead down to its nostrils. Around the slit are tiny flaps of skin that look like leaves.

Slit-faced bats have long arms. At the end of each arm is a hand. Each hand has four fingers and a thumb with a claw. Flight **membranes** stretch between the bat's fingers, body, legs, and tail. There is a T-shaped tip of **cartilage** at the end of the long tail.

The slit-faced bat's short, broad wings help it fly in thick forests. They can fly slowly and quickly. This helps them snatch insects from the surface of trees and plants.

Bat Anatomy

ARMS

THUMB

FINGERS

WING
MEMBRANE

EAR

LEG

NOSE

TAIL

FEET

SENSES

Slit-faced bats have ears that are longer than their head. So, these bats have excellent hearing. They can also see, taste, and feel things. They have another sense, too. It is called echolocation. Bats use echolocation to "see" in the dark.

To use echolocation, slit-faced bats make high-pitched sounds. These sounds bounce off objects such as trees, buildings, and insects.

The sound returns to the bat as an echo. The bat uses the echo to tell how far away things are. The echo can also tell bats how big an object is.

Slit-faced bats use hearing and echolocation to find food. They also use it to find their way around. Sometimes, they use echolocation to avoid danger!

Sound wave sent out by bat

Echo wave received by bat

DEFENSE

Some animals think a slit-faced bat makes a tasty meal. Owls and hawks like to eat slit-faced bats. So do snakes and other **mammals**, including bigger bats!

Slit-faced bats stay safe during the day by staying in their **roost**. But, **predators** often lurk outside their roosting place. They grab the bats as they leave at dusk and return at dawn.

Slit-faced bats use echolocation to avoid being captured. They also use their flying skills to avoid birds of **prey**. Only a skilled predator can catch a healthy slit-faced bat!

Egyptian slit-faced bats avoid predators by roosting in papyrus swamps.

Food

Slit-faced bats must work to avoid **predators**. But they are predators, too. Slit-faced bats eat insects, moths, and butterflies.

These insects sit on lighted walls or on leaves. So, slit-faced bats often fly around lighted areas. Humans often provide bats with fine hunting spots. Streetlights or lighted store signs attract insects at night. Slit-faced bats swoop down and feast on these insects.

But, insects aren't their only **prey**. Some slit-faced bats have been known to eat other bats. Others eat spiders and scorpions. Still others catch and eat fish, frogs, and birds.

Bats eat many insects and other pests that bother people and harm crops. So, their human neighbors benefit when bats hunt. This makes slit-faced bats an important part of the **ecosystem**.

Some scholars believe the slit in a slit-faced bat's face helps it use echolocation when hunting.

BABIES

In order to continue contributing to Earth's **ecosystem**, slit-faced bats must reproduce. The bats have breeding seasons in both the spring and the fall. The babies are born about five months later.

Female slit-faced bats usually have just one baby. A baby bat is called a pup. The pup is born alive. It is quite large when it is born. Some pups are one-quarter of the size of their mother at birth! Their thumbs and hind feet are almost adult sized at birth. This helps them cling to their mother or to their **roost**.

The pups drink their mother's milk for up to two months. Meanwhile, the pups hitch rides on their mothers as they fly. After about two months, a slit-faced bat pup is full grown.

A slit-faced bat mother carries her newborn pup along as she flies. When the pup grows too heavy to carry, she will leave it at the roost.

GLOSSARY

cartilage (KAHR-tuh-lihj) - the soft, elastic connective tissue in the skeleton. A person's nose and ears are made of cartilage.

ecosystem (EE-koh-sihs-tuhm) - a community of organisms and their environment.

family - a group that scientists use to classify similar plants or animals. It ranks above a genus and below an order.

habitat - a place where a living thing is naturally found.

isolate - to separate from something.

mammal - an animal with a backbone that nurses its young with milk.

membrane - a thin, easily bent layer of animal tissue.

muzzle - an animal's nose and jaws.

nocturnal (nahk-TUHR-nuhl) - active at night.

outcrop - the part of a rock formation that projects out of the ground.

pollinate - when birds and insects transfer pollen from one flower or plant to another.

predator - an animal that kills and eats other animals.

prey - animals that are eaten by other animals; also the act of seizing prey.

roost - a place, such as a cave or a tree, where bats rest during the day; also, to perch.

species (SPEE-sheez) - a kind or type.

wingspan - the distance from one wing tip to the other when the wings are spread.

WEB SITES

To learn more about slit-faced bats, visit ABDO Publishing Company on the World Wide Web at **www.abdopub.com**. Web sites about bats are featured on our Book Links page. These links are routinely monitored and updated to provide the most current information available.

INDEX